THE ART OF
BALANCING
BURNOUT

With love,

Vanessa Autrey

THE ART OF

BALANCING

BURNOUT

VANESSA AUTREY

Cover illustration designed by
Mihail ©

Vanessa Autrey

Saint Petersburg, Florida

2021

First paperback edition November 2021

Library of Congress Control Number: 2021922542

Published by Vanessa Autrey ©
www.vanessaautrey.com
hello@vanessaautrey.com

Vanessa Autrey

The Art of Balancing Burnout

ISBN: 978-1-7377256-6-4

Cover artwork designed by Mihail ©

Manufactured in the United States of America

Vanessa Autrey

To Mac, who has lovingly accepted me in all of my forms, and inspired me to live life to the fullest.

CONTENTS

"Next to love,

balance is the most important thing."

– John Wooden

INTRODUCTION

For a long time, balance has been viewed as a mystical unicorn that only appears when you've reached work-life nirvana. It's been preached from the self-help pulpits for years, yet even today so many individuals are more tired, worn out, and frustrated than ever before.

Burnout is plaguing our society. Many suffer in silence, occasionally inserting micro-doses of inspiration that spark hope, but that hope eventually fades as the daily demands of life rear their sweet ugly heads once again.

Some of the most brilliant people I know battle burnout. They wrestle daily with this desire to give life their best, and give it their all. The problem is, most of us forget to take care of ourselves along the way.

We spread ourselves rail thin. We tell ourselves we can handle it - but the truth is, as a society we are running out of bandwidth. We're unhinged, and it's having devastating effects on society as a whole.

With that in mind, I took some time to gather practices and philosophies that have helped me on my own journey to guide you from burnout to balance.

Shall we begin?

Chapter 1

TAKING A CLOSER LOOK AT BURNOUT

Burnout means different things to different people. You've probably already conjured up your own definition of what burnout means to you. Burnout is a relative term. Burnout is in the eye of the beholder, so to speak. Burnout is also much more common than you think, especially since the 2020 global pandemic rocked many of our lives to the core.

Burnout is a newer coined term being tossed around by working professionals, stay-at-home-parents, and the scientific community alike. A lot of folks are trying to better understand it, mainly because a growing number of folks are battling with it each day. Everyone wants to know what causes burnout, and more importantly, what can be done to prevent it.

We all have our own personal experiences with burnout. In its simplest form, burnout happens when an individual is exposed to high levels of stress for prolonged periods. Essentially, that stress accumulates, compounds, and never really finds a proper release. We all have a general responsibility for everything that it takes to live and survive in this world. But when you combine the responsibilities of life, whether it be work, or home, or tasks, or to do's - and things keep adding up - well, it can feel a bit like drinking through a fire hose. The combination of demands, roles, and responsibilities can be a lot sometimes.

Burnout is a fairly new term, conceptualized in the 1970's by American psychologist Herbert Freudenberger. The term burnout was initially created to illustrate the consequences of severe stress and high ideals in helping professions. For example, doctors and nurses, who continually sacrificed themselves for others, would often end up being "burned out" - exhausted, listless, and unable to cope.[1] Nowadays, the term is not only used for those in helping professions, or for the dark side of self-sacrifice. Today, burnout can affect anyone: from working moms and entrepreneurs, to overworked employees and homemakers alike.

Burnout affects each of us a bit differently, but the causes are generally the same. In my opinion, burnout typically occurs when you're one or all of the following: overloaded, overstimulated, and overwhelmed.

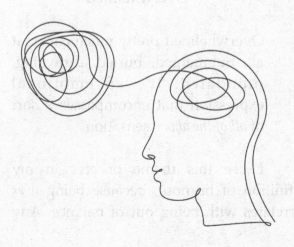

Overloaded

Overloaded means we're spread too thin. We're functioning beyond our own capacity and strength. We're stressed, stretched, and strained.

Overstimulated

Overstimulation happens when we're swamped by more experiences, responsibilities, sensations, noise, and activity than we can cope with. It's sensory overload, and our brains can't quite process the inbound fast enough.

Overwhelmed

Overwhelmed pretty much covers it all. Submerged, buried, drowning, inundated. It's an emotional expression that encompasses a sort of *all of the above* sensation.

I use this theme of *over* in my definition of burnout, because being *over* correlates with being out of balance. Any time you're *over*, chances are you've gone too far. More to come on this in a bit.

Understanding the Causes

In 2020, we experienced a global pandemic that rocked us. People were afraid to step outside, refused to make human contact, and there was always this looming sense of 'what if.' As a society, we're constantly bombarded with with war, natural disasters, political polarization, racism, and civil unrest like never before. Presently in the United States, I would argue that our country is more divided than we have ever been. Expand your view globally, and you discover China's Social Credit System. Grab your smartphone, and now you've got the influences of social media and the feelings of inadequacy, dissatisfaction, and isolation that it breeds. Rewind it back to 1992 when smartphones were released. This constant connectivity has led to a newer concept of availability culture, essentially being available 24/7. While technology has been a great societal accelerator, never have we been more connected to the world and disconnected from ourselves.

For those of us who live in a city, the average person sees more people in a day than our great grandparents did in a year. We're faced with this constant bombardment and social exhaustion, not to mention the newly awkward social distancing that has also disconnected us from many of our communal needs, like hugs and human contact.

The work-from-home shift created this new lack of separation between work and home, which ultimately made stepping away difficult. Working from home has blurred the lines of work-life balance, and many folks are struggling to make it through the day-to-day.

Various independent studies have concluded that the great majority of us are struggling with burnout, mental health, and work-life balance - even if we're not totally aware of it. Many people in our lives are downright miserable, just going through the motions to get to the next day. Many of us have stopped paying attention to our own needs. It's not because we aren't aware of them, it's just that we can't seem to find the time to properly tend to them.

The news doesn't help: bombarding us with tragedies, negative happenings, and end of the world insinuations. If you're a business owner - forget about it. Do you meet your prospective client for coffee? If you decide to meet them, do you shake their hand or is that weird now? Are you uncomfortable, not knowing how to fully express your opinion for fear of the new "cancel culture" that has developed in our society? Like the moment you disagree with someone politically all of the sudden you're Hitler? Give me a break.

I mean really... socially, politically, career-wise, family-wise - it's all scrambled together. Messy, chaotic, disorder - at least in my little world. I know a lot of folks, myself included, who simply don't have enough bandwidth to make it through the day with the demands we're faced with. We're spread too thin, our tanks are on E; we're totally guilty of doing too many things at once, all while trying to manage the noise in our heads that says we're not doing enough.

We're facing a lot of pressure and it all sounds a bit depressing, doesn't it? I'm sure you're no stranger to the day-to-day, mundane rigmarole. Maybe you're a professional life handler - and you just keep on trudging through, holding it all together. Good for you. I've been there too - crushing it, crushing life, but eventually - burnout caught up with me, and we'll explore my breaking point in the next chapter.

The Consequences of Burnout

When we boil burnout down to its core, it's less about how you get there and more about what happens afterward. The consequences of burnout are dire and the aftereffects are destroying our health, happiness, and our quality of life.

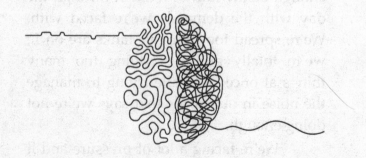

If you're feeling burnt out, it is not just a feeling that will go away on its own. Neuroscientists, and the awesome folks at The Science of People have discovered that burnout has the following effects on your brain[2]:

- It enlarges your amygdala – the part of the brain that controls emotional reactions. This can increase moodiness. It also causes you to have a stronger stress response when startled.

- Burnout causes the prefrontal cortex – the part of the brain that is responsible for cognitive functioning – to thin. This happens normally with aging, but in people who are stressed for prolonged periods, it occurs much more rapidly.

- Parts of the brain that control memory and attention spans are weakened. This makes it more difficult to learn.

- The brains of chronically burnt-out people show similar damage as people who have experienced trauma.

- Burnout reduces the connectivity between different parts of the brain which can lead to decreased creativity, working memory, and problem-solving skills.

Prolonged exposure to stress not only affects your brain, but it takes a toll on the rest of your body too. It has been medically proven that prolonged exposure to stress can cause or exacerbate the following[3]:

- Mental health problems: depression, anxiety, and personality disorders

- Cardiovascular problems: heart disease, high blood pressure, abnormal heart rhythms, heart attacks, and stroke

- Obesity and other eating disorders

- Sexual dysfunction: impotence and premature ejaculation in men and loss of sexual desire in both men and women

- Skin and hair problems: acne, psoriasis, eczema, and permanent hair loss

- Gastrointestinal problems: gastritis, ulcerative colitis, and irritable colon

Conclusively, we all know that burnout is bad. We know that some stress is okay, but a lot of stress is damaging. It's important to understand what burnout does to our brains, our health, and our lives so we can take proactive steps to avoid what happens beyond, like an unfortunate encounter with bandwidth overload, also known as your breaking point.

Chapter 2

BANDWIDTH OVERLOAD

According to a Greek legend, in ancient
Athens a man noticed the great storyteller
Aesop playing childishly with a group of
young boys. The man laughed and jeered
at Aesop, asking him why he wasted his
time in such frivolous activity.

Aesop responded by picking up a
bow, loosening its string, and placing it on
the ground. Then he said to the critical
Athenian, *"Now, answer the riddle if you can.
Tell us what the unstrung bow implies."*

The man looked at it for several
moments but had no idea what point
Aesop was trying to make. Aesop

explained, "*If you keep a bow always bent, it will break eventually; but if you let it go slack, it will be more fit for use when you want it.*" [4]

I think people are a bit like that too.

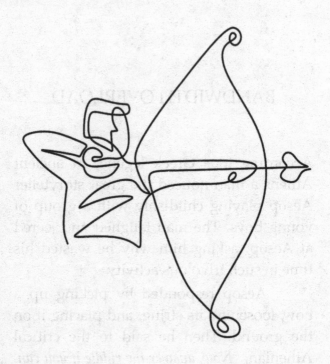

You see, human beings are incredible. We really are. Our creativity, our genius, our resilience - it's astounding. We really are amazing with grand lives to live, great purposes to fulfill, and great stories to tell. On the flip side, we are still human - finite, and fragile at times too. I know some people who do a rockstar job managing extreme stress, but even superheroes have to take off their cape every now and again.

I guess what I'm trying to say is... we all have a breaking point. I believe in you - and I know you can do anything, but you can't do everything all the time. You can't be everywhere all the time, and you can't be everything to everyone all the time either.

My Breaking Point + the Inspiration for This Book

When the pandemic devastatingly struck our globe, it changed life as I knew it. I had gone from traveling across the state for work to being glued to my desk and computer screen. I had an application installed by my company that enabled a chat function via Microsoft Teams. I was used to communicating the old school way: either by email, phone, or text. If I was in a meeting and you called, you'd get a callback later. If I wanted to step out and grab lunch, there was no guilt or fear attached. But once that live chat feature was installed, I felt this paralyzing responsibility to sit at my computer all the day long. If I left the screen idle, even for 5 minutes, it would clock my time away. That meant my manager could see that I wasn't at my desk, and therefore not working, and now my job is at risk.

At first, working from home was fun; meetings in my pajama bottoms with a hot cup of tea conveniently waiting for my attention. I could pop in a load of laundry in between conference calls, and tackle housework throughout the day to free up my evenings. The stress eventually started to grow when I realized there were no clear boundaries between my work and my life. I felt like I was always on, especially because my manager required our camera to be on at all times. While I understood that everyone was doing the best they could to adjust and adapt to the changes - I felt my employer wasn't making big strides or adjustments to focus on the well-being of their employees. I wasn't the only employee who felt that way, and often found myself being the sounding board for disgruntled colleagues and co-workers dealing with their own stress and frustrations. The culmination of all the work drama made me angry, cynical, and a bit bitter too.

I had always been the positive, persevering, 'it's going to be alright' employee, but my enthusiasm eventually faded. The work toxicity bled its way into my marriage, my family, and my friendships. I was always tired - and not depressed tired - I just didn't have the bandwidth to do more than I was doing. And all I seemed to be doing was work-work, or house-work, or wife-work, or life-work. Eventually, family time felt more like an obligation rather than something I enjoyed. Not because of my values, but simply because I was spread too thin. I had this mindset of more, harder, better, faster but the truth was, I was spinning out of control.

The breaking point for me - and the day I realized how big the burnout problem was in my own life - was the day I almost committed suicide. I considered it before but that once small voice had gotten louder, life had gotten messier, and to be honest - I guess I felt ending my life was the only way out. Work and life, and the blurry lines in between had gotten so overwhelming that I thought maybe, just maybe, that would solve it all.

And while suicide is never the answer, sometimes it does feel like an option - especially when you're overloaded and looking to escape from the chaos of life. And that's all I really wanted - was a break from all the mayhem simply to breathe.

Now I share that very sensitive, very honest detail with you so you understand where I'm coming from. I'm not a literary scholar or an award-winning psychologist observing you through the looking glass. I've done research to build my case, but the reality is: I'm right here with you - I'm in the trenches of day-to-day life *with you* and my advice is coming from a place of personal experience, perseverance and growth. My breaking point is what inspired me to take action and help folks just like you balance burnout too.

Balancing Burnout

Deep down inside I knew that suicide wasn't the answer. It wasn't something I could actually go through with, but the thought had crossed my mind. No, I'm not crazy. No, I don't need psychological intervention. No, I didn't make any actual attempts to take my own life. What I am very familiar with though, is wrestling with the feeling that life - the chaos, the disorder, the confusion - can simply be too much sometimes. It was a mess, all in my head, all at one time.

The pressures of life have been constant for many of us. The world can be a lot to handle, and a lot to take in some days. At the pace most of us move, it's essential to have burnout balancing practices, and philosophies that keep us on track. With that in mind, I spent some time gathering 12 practices and 7 philosophies that I personally put into action to live a more balanced life. I have found them to be tremendously helpful on my own journey - I hope they help you too.

Chapter 3

GETTING TO KNOW YOURSELF
AGAIN

Before we dive into burnout balancing practices and life-changing philosophies, I'd like you to explore getting to know yourself again.

Who are you? No, really. Are you an entrepreneur? A CEO? A student? Are you an artist, or a nurse, or a mom, or maybe all three? Maybe you're a single dad barely making ends meet. Are you a daughter, or a son, or a sister, or a friend? Are you performance-oriented? Do you define yourself by your successes? What about your failures?

Just between the two of us... are you happy?

I wasn't. And not because I didn't have anything to be happy about. My life, outside of work, was actually pretty perfect. I knew that, which is what frustrated me even more. I had every reason in the world to be vibrant and full of life - but I wasn't. I was so caught up in the whirlwind around me that I lost my sense of gratitude and my wellbeing along the way.

You see, knowing who you are is essentially the first step in knowing your needs. And trust me, knowing your needs is a critical factor in your ability to balance burnout on a day-to-day basis.

Here's An Example to Illustrate

I'm a wife, daughter, sister, friend, and dog mom of one. I'm a chef, and a maid. I'm an entrepreneur, a CEO, and a student of life. I work a 9-5 job in corporate America - so I'm an employee too. I'm also an artist. I'm a perfectionist, performance-oriented, and

I most certainly - at least in the past - have defined myself by my successes, and my failures. I've got a lot going for me, and a lot going on.

In the past, I prided myself on my ability to keep all the plates spinning, and for the most part did a pretty great job not dropping them. But eventually, I dropped the plates one by one. I was spread so thin in some areas that I couldn't show up fully to others. My 9-5 job in corporate America was one of the biggest vampires in my life - not because I worked with a bunch of Draculas, but because I had a really poor sense of what true balance was.

I was so caught up in the performance aspect of that job; I ultimately neglected my marriage, my friendships, my family, and even my passions (like writing and painting). I was just so tired all the time - and not physically, just mentally exhausted from being overloaded, overstimulated, and overwhelmed. I liked who I was, but didn't like how I was - if that makes sense.

Bottom line, I knew I couldn't go on the way I had been living. I also really didn't have the option to put any of my plates down.

I really liked my husband, so I vowed to keep him. I also really liked my dog, so I kept him too. I would always be a daughter, and sister, but definitely needed to make more of an effort in the friend zone. I loved cooking, and found release in that. I believe in the power of learning, and would never relent on my quest as a student of life. I couldn't exactly quit my 9-5 job, and even if I did, part of me wanted to accept that challenge as a way of connecting with other folks wrestling with burnout. After all, how could I encourage you to find your strength and stick it out if I told you, "quit, there's something better out there." I'm not a quitter, and I don't think you are either.

With that in mind, I picked up my plates, and decided to keep them spinning because I wanted to experience the strife, and busyness of life. I wanted to learn the art of balancing burnout once and for all, and this is what I've come up with so far.

Knowing Your Needs

Part of knowing yourself is knowing your needs. A need is a requirement, a necessity - it is irrevocably essential to your survival, your health, and your wellbeing.

The last section gave us a pretty good idea of our roles and responsibilities in life, but what do you need? Are you an introvert? Extrovert? Ambivert? What are your hobbies? What are you passionate about? What are your gifts? What excites you? What frustrates you? What eases your frustration? How often do you ease your frustration?

I had a good idea of what my own needs were, however, I hadn't done a good job tending to them. I was always jumping to the needs of others, or the demands of my job that I had fallen deep into a state of self-neglect.

My needs have been consistent throughout life: I'm an ambivert, which means sometimes I'm social but sometimes I prefer solitude. I'm an artist at heart, so I find release in writing and painting. I was raised in an Italian home, so cooking is an avenue where I find comfort and expression. I don't like loud noises, and I can get overstimulated by noise easily. I need a good 30-minute walk daily. I also never start my day without a gigantic steamy cup of Zen green tea. I have a morning ritual - light a candle, pour a cup of tea, pray, practice yoga - then and only then am I ready to start my day. I also really enjoy reading philosophy, and self-help books. I'm adventurous, so I need a hint of spontaneity from time to time too. Spending time in nature is essential, at least a few times each week. I also sometimes just like to sit in silence - a sort of, dolce far niente if you please.

It's a long list and you might be thinking 'What a complicated creature,' but the truth is, if you take some time to self-explore, you'd uncover that you have your own list of needs too. Maybe some of my needs overlap with your own. Maybe your list isn't quite as long, or maybe it's a bit longer. To be honest, it doesn't really matter. What you need is what you need, and that's okay.

Knowing Your Limits

My corporate job was in sales, so I spent most of my day in meetings. My husband is an extrovert, so I spent most of my evenings speaking with him. I would fill in my breaks with a quick call to my mom or dad or mother-in-law, maybe swing by my Noni's place. My husband and I were both working from home, which meant cooking wasn't limited to dinner - it was breakfast, lunch, and dinner for 2, every... single... day. I love my dog, but working from home, I quickly learned how obnoxious a 100-pound German Shepherd bark can be. I live in the city, so there's hustle and bustle all around me. My corporate job was crushing me between a high sales quota, and daily Zoom trainings of our new product suite. My co-workers would call me to vent and complain. I had endless projects, and business ideas, and dreams, and goals. We had a death in our family and on top of it all - the pandemic was still a very real part of our day-to-day lives.

The only quiet time I found was getting up at 5 in the morning, essentially beating the world to the punch, but I also had a hard time functioning once 3 o'clock rolled around. A lot was going on, and I felt crushed under the pressure. Any moment of free time was filled with a task, or a to-do. It was suffocating.

Now, you already read about my breaking point earlier - yeah, that part when I thought about taking my life. I reiterate just to illustrate - we (*my sweet husband and I*) had a lot going on. We had met our limit, we just didn't know it. We were functioning in a state of super stress. We pushed ourselves beyond the point of burnout, whatever that's called. It was a lot - simply too much. And once you find yourself buried in all the mess, it's a lot harder to pull yourself out.

Upon eventually digging ourselves out, I resolved that it'd make more sense to treat myself a bit better, know my needs more intimately, know my limits more clearly, and practice self-care more relentlessly so life wouldn't get so out of control, ever again.

I offer that same advice to you now. Knowing your limits gives you a set of boundaries. They allow you to see more clearly when you're approaching that state of being *over*. Think of your limits as guide-posts in your life; like if you venture too far beyond, danger lies ahead. And for all my rule-breaking, limit-pushers out there; while it's okay to venture beyond every once in a while, I'm only suggesting you don't make it a habit with your health. I don't like to feel caged any more than the next person, but the key to finding your balance is cultivating self-awareness. You cultivate self-awareness by knowing yourself more closely, knowing your needs more intimately, and knowing your limits more clearly.

Chapter 4

FINDING YOUR BALANCE

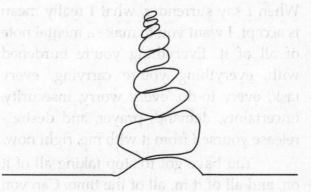

This is the chapter where I think you'll start to feel better. We're going to explore this idea of balance, what it means, how to find it, grab it, and never let it go. Think of this chapter as an opportunity to disconnect, pause, reflect, observe, and recalibrate your way into a healthier, more balanced, more full life.

Things have been hectic, and chaotic, and flying all around you. Believe me when I say, I understand. Maybe we haven't wrestled with exactly the same things - but life is a bit messy nonetheless. That's good - messy is good. Messy is a great starting point. It's also the perfect place to surrender.

Yep - I want you to surrender to all the things going on in your life right now. When I say surrender, what I really mean is accept. I want you to make a mental note of all of it. Everything you're burdened with, everything you're carrying, every task, every to-do, every worry, insecurity, uncertainty, demand, prayer, and desire - release yourself from it with me, right now.

You have got to stop taking all of it on, and all of it in, all of the time. Can you accept that things are a bit messy in your life? Can you be okay with it? In case no one taught you this, you don't have to have all the answers, all the time. You don't have to have it all figured out today.

You don't have to be more than exactly who you are in this moment. Okay?

And if in this moment you're a little frazzled, a little frustrated, and life is a little messy - take a deep breath in, hold it, and then let it all go. Accept yourself for who you are. Accept your life for where it is. Trust me when I say, it's all going to be okay.

What Comes After Acceptance?

Alright. So, you're a self-confessed burnout with a messy life, and now you're 4 chapters deep in a book written by a no-name author who may have actually figured this balance thing out.

So how in the world do we achieve this ever-so-fleeting, unicorn thing called balance? And I mean really getting it, grasping it and making balance your own. This is more than reading an inspirational blog post, or adding this book to your self-help collection after you've finished. Refuse to fall into the old shenanigans you're used to. I'm talking about a self-discovered balance that truly drives lasting change. I want you to step outside of your comfort zone - reach deep within, and really make a vow to yourself that you deserve this.

What Is Balance, Anyway?

The first step is always the hardest, right? Or maybe you've taken a few steps before but somewhere along the way, still found yourself overwhelmed, and a little out of control. Believe me when I say, it's okay to begin again. And I hope by now, at least from what you've read, you are more committed than ever to discover your own version of balance. It's within your reach, and it's within your power too. You deserve it.

So what does balance mean? And what does it look like in practice? Well, I think it's safe to say the definition is evolving. For a long time, balance had this work-life notion attached to it. The world has changed. Ideals have changed. People's lives, and lifestyles have changed too.

To put it quite simply, though, balance is the equilibrium of everything you have on your plate - whatever that looks like for you. Balance is personal; it's the sweet spot, baby - where we can feel good, and feel like we have a better handle on life. Balance is the secret weapon, and true key to creating a sense of happiness, and wellbeing in our lives.

Balance requires a sense of presence, and the art of learning to live in the moment. Balance demands self-awareness to thrive. Balance is recognizing when we're approaching our limit; our *over-the-edge* moment, allowing us to stop and give ourselves proper space and time to recalibrate. It's about having a better impact on everything we touch. It's about having a positive impact on our children, friend's, and family's lives. Balance is about prioritizing what's important to you without the societal guilt of practicing self-care. It's about having better boundaries that you feel confident enforcing. It's all of these things and more importantly, it's the epiphany that you don't have to be everything to everyone all the time.

Balance also boils down to contentment. Contentment is a state of happiness, but I take it a step further. I think contentment boils down to personal peace. It's a state of mind where you're at ease. There could be a whirlwind going on around you, and although these things are happening, you don't have to let them in.

For example, after my breaking point, I had to take it easy. I really had no other choice in the matter, because physically, I knew my body couldn't take much more. I didn't start doing a worse job or forget my sales quota, or my husband, or my dog, or anything else really - I guess I just stopped letting it all in, all at once. I stopped believing the lie of perfectionism. I stopped giving everything so much power in my life.

I would tell myself things like, "It's just a job," and "don't take it too seriously." And, so I didn't. Little by little over time, rather than dramatically quitting or blowing my top, I decided to show up, accept where things were at, and remind myself that this too shall pass. Like a gentle reminder that though some storms come into our lives, they don't last forever. This, like many of the other storms I had been through, would pass too. Eventually, the fog would lift, and I'd be able to see clearly again.

I learned that nothing good comes from over-expressing your emotions. I also learned that our emotions are very fickle, ever-changing things. We can make mountains out of molehills, and have ourselves believing life truly sucks.

Life doesn't suck - you're probably just tired. When is the last time you took a nap? When is the last time you did something just for yourself? Therein lies the problem. My sense of being overloaded, overstimulated, and overwhelmed was simply the result of my own negligence, and lack of commitment to self-care.

We read these inspirational articles online and think to ourselves, 'hey, I can do that.' But when the rubber meets the road, most of the time our self-commitments fall by the way-side, because something we think is more important comes along. Our good intentions become background noise to the chaos of life.

Balance is as much a necessity as the food you eat, the water you drink, and the air you breathe. Balance is not a luxury to the life-hackers of our time. For the cynics, balance is not impossible. I know this because people can change the things they want to change in their lives. It really just boils down to the commitment, will-power, and realization that balance belongs to you too. Balance is essential, and belongs to each and every one of us, we just have to create it for ourselves.

On that note, we've touched on surrender and acceptance to the messiness of life. We've determined that balance is the sweet spot, and the key to living a happier, fuller life. We've uncovered how essential balance is. I'd also like to clarify that balance isn't about achieving some state of unrealistic perfection. It's about discovering sustainable practices to help keep your life priorities in check.

When work becomes too big, pull yourself back. When you find yourself drowning in thoughts and anxieties about things beyond your control, pull yourself back. When you're getting a little too out of hand on the pleasure spectrum (naughty you), pull yourself back. You've got to notice when you've gone too far in one part of your life, and simply pull yourself back. Does that make sense?

Imagine your sweet, beautiful self at the center. And you have all the wonderful parts of your life around you - your family, your health, your friendships, your career, and so forth. They all revolve around you, and without you these things would not be. Some days, some things will demand more attention than others. That's alright. What we want to avoid is one part getting more attention, for a prolonged time period to where the other parts of you suffer. Too much of anything can be a bad thing, and so the key to adopt is *everything in moderation*.

Yes, indeed. It boils down to moderation. Take your stress in moderation. Take your job in moderation. Take your children (*as best you can*) in moderation. Train your inner ear to listen to your needs a bit more. When you feel yourself spiraling, or notice you're more ornery than usual - use those as your indicators that you're out of balance. Take a break, take a step back, observe, breathe, recalibrate.

I just have to say, I'm so proud of you. You've come this far and you're still with me, still engaged, still reading. The fact that you're still here tells me you're going to knock this balance thing out of the park. I'm genuinely excited to be on this journey with you. I'm here to remind you who you are, and also to tell you: you've got this baby!

Shall we continue?

Chapter 5

12 PRACTICES FOR BALANCING BURNOUT

Okay - so we know ourselves a bit better now. We're self-confessed burnouts, who are committed to improving our quality of life. Dare I say we're well on our way!

With that in mind, I put together a list of practices that have tremendously helped me evolve from a stressed-out thirty-something into a living, breathing, thriving human being. They are called practices, namely because they require some action on your part. None of these will produce any value in your life until you put them into action. You can pick and choose as you please - you can even create your own. I encourage you to incorporate at least 3 of them into your daily life, and watch them draw you closer to more balanced living.

One: *Take* Micro-Breaks
Throughout the Day

Micro-breaks stimulate productivity. No, really. It's scientifically proven. What is a micro-break you may ask? It's exactly what it sounds like; a short break you take from your stuff during the day.

If you're a hustling-bustling CEO, step away for a few every now and then. If you're a stay-at-home mom bogged down with chores and mini-me demands, create 5 minutes here and there to enjoy a cup of tea and recharge those batteries. Stand up. Stretch. Go for a quick walk. Step outside for a breath of fresh air. Micro-breaks are really whatever tickles your fancy. The key is to take micro-breaks and take them often. If we sit, stand, think, or do too often - our energy gets stuck. We become stagnant and lose a bit of our creativity. It's unnatural - so learn to step away every now and again for a micro-break to catch your breath and keep your sanity.

Two: *Ditch* the To-Do List
Once In A While

Next up is occasionally ditching that to-do list. Yes, that long checkbox-looking piece of paper sitting on your desk or kitchen counter right now.

You know the one... that never-ending home-improvement list, or chores, or what you need for your upcoming college applications. Yep, I'm talking about that checklist of your business ideas, and aspirations too. The checklist of work demands, and priorities that just keeps growing. Once in a great while, just ditch the darn list!

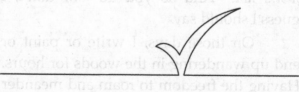

Don't get me wrong, lists are great. I'm a list-writer myself, mainly because I'm a Type-A perfectionist psycho that doesn't want anything to fall through the cracks. I consider myself a get-it-done kind of person. But you know what, sometimes, I just have to look the other way. Mainly because I now know that those lists never end. Every day will bring its own trouble and sometimes we need to drop it all and simply live in the moment.

That being said, put yourself higher on your own to-do list. Making myself a priority has helped balance out all the chaos going on in my head. It's taught me to let go once in a while and just be. I've learned to savor those days. They tend to be the most satisfying, especially when you're on the edge of burnout, even more so when you're beyond it.

It's sort of like, *"Yes, I know... I could be writing my next book or climbing that mountain, but today seems like a good day to just... not!"* And so you do - or don't, I guess I should say.

On those days, I write or paint or end up wandering in the woods for hours. Having the freedom to roam and meander through the day - even just a part of the day, can be so very nurturing. I believe we should all make time for undirected activity that is our own. Our own expression, our own creation, and most importantly - our own control.

By ditching the to-do list for a day here and there, you're giving yourself permission to do as you please. As we each discovered in the previous sections, needs vary from person to person. The one common thread is that we all need a little me-time sprinkled throughout our lives. By ditching the to-do list once in a while, we can accomplish it.

Ditching the to-do list isn't a permanent solution. By no means am I saying to-do lists are bad. I'm simply saying: once in a while it's okay to let loose. It's okay to snatch back some of your independence and do what you want. Not all of us can afford the luxury of free time to do this every day, after all, we have goals to accomplish, places to be, and people to meet. But, we all can afford a day here and there where we say - forget the to-do list and have our own day.

Three: *Have* Your Perfect Day

Here's an exercise I encourage you to try:
imagine your perfect day. What does that
look like for you? Think outside the box. If
you woke up tomorrow and could create
your own perfect day, what would it look
like?

Would you sleep in? Would you stay
in your PJs all day? Would you read or
write or paint? Would you go for a hike or
head down to the beach? What would you
eat? Do you have a favorite cafe? What
would you drink? No structure, just
pleasure. Just ask yourself, *"what do I want
in this moment?"*

For me, I'd get up when my body
woke up. I'd have a nice steamy cup of
Zen green tea with extra honey, of course.

Once I went through my morning meditation session, I'd throw on my yoga pants (*because on my perfect day, no other pants exist*), and head down to my favorite French bakery for a fresh butter croissant. I'd walk down to the marina, and marvel at the beautiful yachts parked in the bay. I'd meander and ponder. No headphones, no agenda, absolutely no cell phone - just wandering through the day. I'd pick up some fresh flowers, tasty cheese, and exotic wine. I'd head home, take a nice hot bath surrounded by beeswax candles, and eucalyptus steam. I'd have an afternoon cup of tea, grab my next read, and get lost in a book for a bit. Later on, I'd uncork that bottle of wine, cut that cheese, and have a little charcuterie party for 1. At that point, I'd probably be ready for some company - so maybe I'd invite my husband to join in on the spread.

I know some folks whose perfect day would consist of hitting the ski slopes or skydiving. I know others who would hang in their pajamas, watch movies, and order takeout. I know some who would fish, boat, or hike. Different strokes for different folks - it's healthy, it's normal, it's *good*!

The idea here is to imagine your perfect day then go live it out once in a while. It couples with ditching your to-do list every now and then. The key is simply to do whatever you want! We can't wait until the kids are grown, or retirement, or our next vacation, or until our bank account has a certain number of zeros. Tomorrow is promised to no one; so be sure and take time to enjoy life today!

Four: *Find* An Outlet

Let's face it: most of us are pent up - we really are. Maybe you're pent up, and you don't even know it. I've been there in both my personal life, and my professional career. The days where the work, and tasks, and demands just pile up until you're about to explode, or even worse, implode. The insane pressure placed on us by our jobs, coupled with the societal, familial, and unending pressure we place on ourselves - well it's enough to make anyone lose their marbles.

We can't keep it bottled up inside of us. We also can't explode on our colleagues or the people in our lives. So what do we do with all this pressure and stress that's built up inside of us? We find an outlet.

An outlet is a means of self-expression. It's a way of counteracting our over-worked, over-stressed, over-cooked brains. An outlet gives way to let it out. It's a release of frustration, and an avenue for self-healing and self-care. If you examine the definition closely, one synonym actually refers to an outlet as a "safety valve." Think about that for a second - an outlet is an opening that automatically relieves excessive pressure.

And that's all we really need from time to time - a release from the pent-up frustrations, and pressures we carry around on our shoulders day-to-day.

I'd like to make one thing crystal clear - stop wearing your work-load, and your life-load around like a badge of honor. No one will think less of you if you take a moment for yourself here and there.

The reality is: there will always be more work. From our jobs and owning businesses, to being a manager of our families and our homes - *there will always be more work*. It never goes away. We never escape from the responsibilities that life presents us. But one of our main responsibilities should be ourselves, after all, there's only one of us anyway. We should take some pride in checking in - making sure we're safe, and whole, and okay. Having an outlet helps reset us back to normal. Having an outlet guides us back to balance so we can tackle the realities and responsibilities that life throws our way.

For some, their outlet is writing. For others, it's painting. My husband likes to go fishing, and my mom likes to forage for chaga in the woods. I have friends who draw, and some get lost in nature. My dad sits in his big brown leather chair, listening to his favorite music. Wherever you're at, whatever nurtures you - it's essential that you learn to take some time to rediscover your peace, center yourself, and find your balance once again.

By no means am I saying take a year-long sabbatical - but maybe you take next Friday off for a little you time? Maybe you take a half-day next Wednesday, and go for a walk in the woods. Really take hold of this idea. For your own peace and for your own sanity, understand the importance of nourishing yourself. Learn to pause for a moment and ask yourself:

"what do I need right now?" Really contemplate what a good outlet would be, just for you, and then make time to do it. I can assure you, there will always be more work, and more demands from life, but there is undoubtedly only one you.

Five: *Learn* How to Unplug

We spend so much of our time being available to people, places, and things. While technology has its benefits, it also has tremendous drawbacks if not used in moderation. From the constant screen scrolling and back-to-back conference call sessions, to email checking and social media dings - not to mention the nightly Netflix binge to try and get our mind off of work - well, we're dealing with a lot of screens throughout the day.

Society has promoted technology, and this culture of constant connectivity. Psychologists have been scrambling to gather data to truly understand the debilitating effects this over-use of technology is having on our society.

Here are some theories on how technology affects us:

- Affects our sleeping habits

- Leaves us feeling isolated

- Promotes a more sedentary lifestyle

- Serves as a constant source of distraction

- Leads to neck pain and bad posture

- Promotes a shorter attention span

And the list goes on. The point I'm trying to make is: being plugged in constantly adds a new layer of stress to our lives.

Now, don't get me wrong! I am a proponent of technology, but I also believe in moderation. Most of us are a bit too plugged in, and we need to disconnect for a bit here and there so we can reconnect with ourselves.

You may not be able to walk away from your phone all the time, but you do have opportunities to set your phone aside, take off your iWatch, and have a break. Who cares if you aren't counting your steps or being reminded to breathe. None of your fans or social media followers will miss your life-revealing updates if you step away for a few. You'll find that nature will take its course, you'll keep breathing, and your heart will keep on beating just fine.

Tell yourself - "*I deserve a break today*," and do it. Do it often, every day... multiple times throughout the day if possible, and especially when needed.

The emails, and tasks, and demands will still be waiting for you upon your return - and that's okay. I'm not talking about checking out forever - I'm simply suggesting the occasional break from technology so your brain can breathe.

Something I like to do often is delete social media from my phone! *Insert dramatic gasp.* When I notice my screen time is up 47% over last week, it's likely because I've mindlessly scrolled through Pinterest inspiration trying to make it through Monday's mundaneness.

When I find myself feeling bogged down by technology now, I simply take a break from it. I can't always walk away from work, but I can go for a 30-minute walk, and leave my phone in my office. If my boss calls, I can call them back. If my husband needs me, he'll have to survive for 30 minutes without me. If I had a baby, I'd probably take them with me. What do you call those things anyway? Not the baby but the sling. A Boba. I'd buy one of those, and strap them to my chest - chances are they need some fresh air too.

In all seriousness though, I'm merely suggesting that you give yourself permission to take a break from your screens every now and then. You'll experience the immediate effects of being temporarily unavailable, and I promise you it will feel really, really good.

Six: *Create* Quiet Time

The Harvard Business Review released an interesting article that read: *The Busier You Are, the More You Need Quiet Time*. It was summarized very well, so I'll keep it in its original form: *"Taking time for silence restores the nervous system, helps sustain energy, and conditions our minds to be more adaptive and responsive. For example, silence is associated with the development of new cells in the hippocampus, the key brain region associated with learning and memory. But cultivating silence isn't just about getting respite from the distractions of life. Real sustained silence, the kind that facilitates clear and creative thinking, and quiets inner chatter as well as outer. Try going on a media fast, sitting silently for 2 minutes during the middle of your workday, or taking a long walk in the woods — with no phone. The world is getting louder, but silence is still accessible."* [5]

I love that last part - about how the world is getting louder. It really is. For 6 months out of the year, I live in downtown Saint Petersburg, Florida. The traffic count in front of my office is about 14,000 plus cars a day. When I go on my walks, I encounter 10-20 people. My day job is in sales, essentially constant contact - either with my team, my manager, or my clients. As I mentioned earlier, my husband is an extrovert - so he likes to chat throughout the day too. Oh, and my massive German Shepherd is also a talker, though he's much louder than all of us combined.

I paint this picture to say, my days are very busy and filled with a lot of noise. I don't like a lot of noise or chatter, but it's something I have to cope with daily. I've found ways to cope: quiet time being one of them.

Now since I live in a city, and have a massively obnoxious dog, I do have to use my AirPods. I like to put on a bit of white noise or instrumental piano, and just sit in silence. The blankness allows my mind to tune out the rest of the world - even for just a few moments. I can't hear my email going off, and I intentionally put my phone on Do Not Disturb. My husband knows if my AirPods are in, it's a signal that I'm unavailable. He knows this is my way of recharging throughout the day, and he often does it too. If you have kids and it's hard to escape - might I suggest a nice long tinkle in the bathroom with a strong deadbolt?

I don't have all the answers, but I do know how important it is to quiet my mind throughout the day. We all need to escape from the noise every now and again, and while we can't disappear from life entirely, we can take a break to create our own silence, even if for just a moment here and there.

Seven: *Breathe* Better

I found a few thought-provoking facts about breathing published on The Breath Effect[6] that I thought I'd share:

- The average person breathes in the equivalent of **13 pints of air every minute,** and **takes 17,000 breaths per day**.

- The lungs are the biggest waste removal engine in the body, removing **70% of body waste** in the form of carbon dioxide.

- Psychologists have found that breathing practice is effective in fighting anxiety, depression, and stress. Physiological evidence has indicated that even a single breathing practice significantly reduces blood pressure.

We know that breathing is essential to our survival. Evidence shows its tremendous positive impacts on our health and well-being. I would even go as far to say that breathing exercises can be used as a tool to battle burnout too.

When we're stressed, we habitually tense up. Our shoulders tighten and our breath shortens. While we may be taking the average 17,000 breaths per day, what is the quality of those breaths? Are they deep and long? Are they short and shallow?

As we talk about breathing, take a moment and observe your own breath right now. Maybe you're more relaxed because you've taken some you-time to read this book. Maybe you're frustrated with me because you don't like the woo-woo Yogi talk of breathing "in through the nose and out through the mouth." Either way, I want you to take a deep breath in, hold for a few seconds and then release it. Again - deeply inhale, filling your lungs with air, hold for a few seconds, and slowly release. Do this a few more times and come back to the words on this page.

Do you feel a little calmer, a little more relaxed? Then that's all the proof you need. Breath is an essential part of our nature and effective, intentional breathing can decrease our stress levels, while also improving our mood. The breath is our body's way of beginning again.

I encourage breathing exercises daily - whether your iWatch reminds you to or not. I especially encourage breathing exercises when you're prepping for a big presentation, or just received a frustrating email from your client. Breathe when your toddler is having a major meltdown because you ate the cookie they didn't want. Breathe when your dog chews the furniture, or if the day simply got away from you.

Try a breathing exercise when you first get up in the morning - before you even reach for your phone. Try it before you set out to tackle that to-do list. Try it before you go to sleep at night - maybe make it the last thing you do. Each breathing exercise will take no more than a few minutes. Consider it time well spent on your journey to balance burnout in your life.

Eight: *Check-In* With Yourself

Self-check-ins are a neat yogi trick I learned during my Yoga Teacher Training. It's a mindfulness tool that can be used throughout the day, and you don't need to rattle off in Sanskrit or be able to balance on your head to do them either. The idea is that throughout the day, we tend to rush from moment to moment, meeting to meeting, task to task, and we tend to accumulate residue throughout our day. This in turn can catalyze our stress levels, and negatively affect our quality of life.

When we're caught in the day-to-day momentum, it's easy to say - *"I'm fine, it's just another Monday,"* or whatever excuse we tell ourselves to the stress that silently compounds in our lives. I have found, both through research and personal practice, that a simple 5-minute check-in each day helps slow me down, and rid myself of the buildup in my body and my brain.

So what exactly is a check-in and how do we do it?

A self-check-in is essentially a self-assessment. It's a simple way to gauge where you are at emotionally, energetically, mentally, physically, and spiritually. A check-in isn't a big time commitment, but it does have big personal payoffs. Each go may only take about 5 minutes of your time but will yield tremendous results. Rather than rigidly planning out when you will do your check-in, a good rule of thumb is as soon as you feel yourself getting swept away with the day. Those moments where you start to feel yourself getting overwhelmed with tasks and to-do lists - that is your opportunity.

You can check-in sitting in a chair at your desk or standing up outside. You can do it anywhere, really. I encourage you to silence your phone, and the dinging sound of your inbox - preferably find a place where you can step away from both if possible.

Close your eyes and focus on your breathing. Notice the rise and fall of your breath. Does your breath feel deep or shallow? Can you try to breathe a little bit deeper?

How are you? What's going on in that mind of yours? How do you feel, physically? Are you hungry? Thirsty? How does your neck feel? What about your

61

shoulders? Can you feel your heart beating? Try to become an observer - observe yourself.

How are your thoughts right now? What's on your mind? Okay good, now let it all go.

Continue to breathe deeply, continue to notice, continue to release. No matter what you have going on, meet each experience with acceptance.

And that's it - it's such a simple practice and yet one of my favorites. It takes practically no time, but it is so impactful if done regularly. If you can't do it daily, try a few times a week. Start incorporating this intention of being more mindful with yourself, and your day - you'll recognize the benefits sooner than you think.

Nine: *Spend* Time In Nature

Scientists and researchers are collecting evidence to prove what many of us already know to be true: nature is good for us, and good for our wellbeing.

Think about the building blocks of our bodies - cells. They are dynamic, living units, continually at work towards this process of self-repair and regeneration. Nature can be a major accelerator of this process towards cultivating a better quality of life.

Yale School of the Environment released an interesting study on time spent in nature and its subsequent effects.

"These studies have shown that time in nature — as long as people feel safe — is an antidote for stress: It can lower blood pressure and stress hormone levels, reduce nervous system arousal, enhance immune system function, increase self-esteem, reduce anxiety, and improve mood." [7]

Can you imagine that? Nature has been scientifically proven to counteract the effects of stress. Nature is a true antitoxin to the toxic stress many of us are carrying around each day. So if the cure exists, why do so few of us take time out of our busy lives to enjoy it?

Now chances are you have access to nature, and it's a lot closer than you think. Forests, beaches, mountains, streams, parks, and gardens just to name a few. If you're stuck in the city, Google *"nature park"* or *"butterfly garden."* Whatever glimpse of nature you can find, hold on to it. It may take some hunting to find the right spot, but eventually, you'll find a gem to call your own.

You see, we all need a little escape every now and then. Take time to sit outside and listen to the birds sing - it's melodic. Or go enjoy the sound of the waves crashing on the beach while wiggling your toes in the soft sand. Maybe get up early in the morning and marvel at a sunrise - or wait 'til the days end to appreciate the sunset.

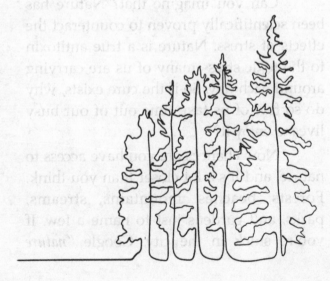

Honestly, it doesn't matter what you do - you just have to find a little slice of nature that works for you. Nature has a way of calming us - demonstrating its power and proving that there's a great, big, beautiful world out there beyond the confines of our office space, to-do lists, and responsibilities of life.

Nature helps put things in proper perspective. Nature is resilient. It's steadfast and evolving. If we pay close enough attention to what nature has to say, we may learn a thing or two about ourselves.

Ten: *Learn* to Live Like the Water

On the subject of nature and self-reflection, I wanted to share a personal experience that took me years to finally understand. My husband and I honeymooned in Bali; a remarkable and unforgettable island. We hired a driver, Wayan (*meaning eldest*) John. Ironically, Wayan John loved John Wayne movies, so we jokingly called him John Wayne. He loved that.

John Wayne wasn't tall, wasn't short - but stout in stature. He had a bald head, brown skin, and was missing a few front teeth. I don't think he was a Yogi or a spiritual guru - he was really just another Balinese native, meandering through life each day. He had an interesting philosophy about work though - as most of the Balinese do. Once he made enough money for the day, he'd usually call it quits and hang out with his buddies for the rest of the afternoon. They'd puff on cigarettes, and enjoy a Bintang beer, but that was about it. There was no rush, no hustle-bustle - no climbing the corporate ladder. They had what they needed, and that was enough.

John Wayne taught us that their traditional Balinese meal was called Nasi Campur - essentially mixed rice, surrounded by side dishes of vegetables and meat. He ate that every morning and every night. He said his wife would occasionally put a fried egg on top of his breakfast, and he really loved that too. He was a simple man and a good contrast to the busy, hectic lives that my husband and I were accustomed to.

I fell in love with the culture and found myself wanting to leave my high-paying sales job to pursue a life of yoga and tranquility in this far away land.

While touring the Balinese countryside, John Wayne uttered 10 really simple, yet profoundly powerful words: *"You must learn to live like the water, my friend."*

Now, maybe he stole that from Bruce Lee's famous **"Be like water"** scene. Regardless, when a bald, toothless Balinese man gives you ancient wisdom, you should probably take it to heart.

I was puzzled at the time. I had little exposure to what many would call The Way, and assumed this was some philosophical jargon I'd understand later in life.

What John Wayne didn't know, was that a few days before our trip to Bali, I suffered a severe nervous breakdown.

Now there's some argument in the scientific community about whether your nerves can actually 'break down,' but until it happens *to* you, I'd advise you not to judge.

That being said, I experienced a full-fledge, uncontrollable, nerve explosion in my $10,000 Yolan Cris wedding gown. I was violently ill; shaking, feverish, vomiting uncontrollably in front of my closest girlfriends and newly wed husband. Rather than dancing the night away, surrounded by our dearest friends and family, my sweet husband held my hair as I hugged the porcelain toilet of our Honeymoon suite.

I guess there was so much compounded stress that had built up within me, it all released at once. I've had bad days, but never like that before, and I hope to never go through it again.

I share that second revealing story to say - I have pushed myself beyond the point of burnout twice. I had taken on too much. I was doing too much. While I appeared fine on the outside, the stress was so repressed that when it finally came out - it destroyed a lot in its path. Looking back, I feel a lot of that could have been avoided. I could have trusted others to hand off a few projects. I could have taken time off of work. I could have asked for help. But I didn't. My perfectionist, Type-A personality wanted it done and I wanted it done right.

Sometimes we get so hellbent on our own vision of the way things "*should be*" - whether a wedding, a career, a family, or a lifestyle. We have this perception that it should look and be a certain way - and when it falls short, we keep pushing, and going, and trying to achieve the perfection that will always elude us.

I realize this practice was supposed to be about *living like the water*. I can see that I've gone off on a bit of a tangent, but this is an important point to grasp. By no means am I discouraging you from the grind - I respect the hustle and am a hustler myself. But some things are beyond our control. The more we try to force them, the more damage we do.

What I'm trying to say is: *there's a lot we can learn from the way water flows*. Water has the ability to adapt, evolve, and become. It melts, it flows, it boils, it steams. Water guides, transforms, challenges, changes, nurtures, and nourishes too. Water does all of this without actually doing anything at all. Water just exists; it just is.

Learning to live like the water teaches us to get into the flow of life... our life. It teaches us how to get out of our own way. It's that idea of going with the flow. I say all that to say, stop trying to be in control of everything all the time. Sometimes we just need to be still, flow, and know.

Eleven: *Cultivate* Gratitude

Gratitude is another powerful practice to balancing burnout. Finding things to be grateful for isn't hard, it's just easy to take them for granted when life is swarming all around you. Gratitude forces us to slow down and notice. It helps bring a sense of awareness and presence into the moment.

So what is gratitude? It's a state of mind - a readiness to show appreciation. Gratitude is a warm feeling of thankfulness towards the world, situations, circumstances, people, and life in general. A person who feels gratitude is thankful for what they have in their lives, and does not require an ounce more for happiness. They are content in their hearts with the way they are, and the way life is around them.

Gratitude is a form of surrender. It is a way of saying: "*I am enough, I have enough*, and *my life is enough*."

Gratitude has consistently been linked to greater happiness, and a more fulfilled sense of wellbeing. Gratitude helps us feel positive emotions, relish good experiences, boost our health, combat adversity, and ultimately build stronger relationships.

Gratitude can be expressed in many ways, but what we want to focus on is cultivating an attitude of gratitude that we can take with us through our day-to-day.

Having an attitude of gratitude can be life-changing. It helps us appreciate what we have, rather than focusing on what we don't. An attitude of gratitude can change your life because it helps to focus on the simplistic beauty around us, and realize the miracle of life within us.

You can practice gratitude at any moment. It's especially beneficial if you find yourself slipping into one of those negativity spirals - maybe someone makes a disrespectful political comment, or your significant other is frustrating you. Maybe you're working from home, while also balancing your kids learning remotely. Whatever the challenge or frustration you're facing, gratitude is a great way to combat, shift, and transform your mindset to a healthier, more balanced one.

So how do we practice gratitude? We simply pause (*stop doing whatever we're doing*), sit still for a moment, and think of a few things to be grateful for. By injecting this pause into our day, we are creating space in our lives to check-in. This is an effective tool for our overall well-being. It allows us to slow down what is happening around us, and cultivate an awareness of what is within.

By stopping this state of being *over*, and focusing on what we're grateful for, we're literally rewiring our brains. Through repetition, and with time - this practice becomes easier, and more natural. Our body will adapt and begin to respond with gratitude more readily when faced with frustration.

What you're grateful for will shift from day to day, but the idea is to focus more on what you do have, and less on what you don't. It's about focusing on what is going right, despite what isn't.

With this practice, you start to notice a softening. Maybe you feel a little less tense - a little less stressed. The softening comes from being able to see the bigger picture - seeing your life through a wider lens. With a mindful intent to focus on gratitude, it enables you to see life from a different perspective - one that is less stressed, less stiff, less frustrated, less pent up.

From there, you've got fertile soil to move forward. You can approach your day with a more clear and calm mind, having taken some time to pause from the frustration you were feeling before.

There's no right or wrong answer to where you go from here. The key is getting away from the automatic responses that lead us down the rabbit hole. We have to be reminded of how important it is to take time throughout the day to do a self-reflection - a check-in on our mental health, and well-being.

Practicing gratitude is a powerful way to help us pause the busyness of our day-to-day lives, and take time to be grateful for our blessings. No matter what's going on around us, we can find a handful of things to be grateful for to shift what's going on within us.

Twelve: *Practice* Relentless Self-Care

My twelfth and final practice in balancing burnout is practicing relentless self-care.

Let me be clear, self-care is not limited to spa days and retreats. It's not a long weekend on the islands, or hiding in the solitude of the mountains. Self-care is a daily commitment to the culmination of your own social, emotional, physical, mental, financial, environmental, and spiritual wellbeing.

Self-care refers to actions and attitudes which contribute to maintaining personal peace, each and every day. It's caring for yourself, and your mental health without the stigma of mental health. It's personal, intimate action to reduce the stress in our lives. It's knowing ourselves, knowing our needs, knowing our limits, and creating our own little version of what it means to be well.

Self-care is for all because it really just boils down to balance. If we find ourselves too heavy on one end of the life spectrum, we create ways to pull ourselves back. Self-care is self-awareness. It's knowing where we're at. When frustrations start to arise, self-care takes a step back and says: *'What's going on here? What do I need?'* and then acts on those needs quickly.

For me, nature has always been a big stress reliever. Something about tucking my phone away, and getting lost in the woods or a trip to the beach to marvel at a sunset has always satisfied my soul. I love a good cup of tea, and a nice hot bath, with Epsom salt of course. My shoulders get a bit kinky so I try to commit to a monthly massage. I love long walks with no destination. I think fresh flowers bring a bit of joy into the home too. I love to put on classical music, and get lost in a good book. I also love grabbing a canvas and some acrylic paint to just let it all out. Sometimes I'll grab charcuterie, wine and have myself a mini picnic - either in my home, at the beach, or on top of a mountain. I've even grabbed cider donuts from the gas station, and sat on a piece of land I wanted to buy.

My husband on the other hand loves video games and fishing. He finds a release in boxing and jiujitsu. He also gets lost in a good book - sometimes for hours on end - but he has his way, in his own world, to meet his own needs. You do too. You have your own way in your own world and your own needs - you just have to realize them and put action behind it.

Self-care doesn't have to be fancy or high-end, or only come once a year when you realize you're on the verge of a nervous breakdown. You don't need to be rich to take care of yourself. You just need to know yourself, know what you need, know your limits, and frequently take a break to *enjoy the little things* in life.

There are more practices out there. These are ones I practice on my own quite often. I hope the twelve I mentioned will be a foundation for you to build upon. I encourage you to explore, and discover your own practices - each of us may have something a little different, and that's okay. Whatever it is - discover what works for you, and make a relentless commitment on your journey toward balancing burnout and better self-care.

Chapter 6

7 PHILOSOPHIES TO ADOPT IMMEDIATELY

Philosophies are equally important to practices. As a matter of fact, they may be more important. Why? Because philosophies are guiding principles for our behavior, and thus our lives. Philosophies give us a sense of direction. They also give us boundaries and guideposts. Once you've adopted a certain philosophy, over time, it becomes natural to you. So what are the 7 philosophies I think you should adopt immediately?

One: Be Less Busy

Busyness is just an excuse. It's like our self-worth armor shouting *"I may not have accomplished everything I want in life, but look how busy I am. I'm going hard, fast, and full-throttle to get there. Just wait, you'll see."*

That's great. Good for you. Not really. When's the last time you stopped to smell the roses? I'm serious. When's the last time you took a moment to appreciate the gift of breathing? How involved are you in your child's life? When's the last time you checked on your friend? And I mean, really asked them how *they* were doing? I don't bring this up to be critical or make you feel judged. Quite the contrary. My goal is to bring a sense of awareness.

Yes, you're busy, but you're not too busy. At the end of the day, people make time for the things they want to make time for. This is true for passions, relationships, and self-care too. You've got to stop viewing your wellbeing as a luxury, and understand that it's as necessary for you as the very air you breathe.

There will always be plenty to do, and you can always pick up from where you left off. All I'm suggesting you drop the busyness facade. Somewhere in between all you have going on, create time and space for yourself - you deserve it.

Two: Discover "Il Dolce Far Niente"

"*Il dolce far niente*" is an Italian expression that translates into *the sweetness of doing nothing*. A beautiful and exotic reminder to find meaning and pleasure in all things. It's about living in the moment, fully and truly. No stress, no pressure; just admiring life in its beauty and simplicity. You appreciate life and you appreciate that you are alive.

The sweetness of doing nothing is all about enjoying yourself. It's a romantic ideal of sweet idleness that is within reach. Pair it with your micro-breaks I mentioned earlier, but adopt it as a philosophy and make it your own.

The key is to do nothing. Create space and time once in a while just to be. Let everything settle, let everything rest; including yourself. Count your blessings. Savor life like you do your favorite meal. Savor the memories. Savor the moment, the time, the noise, the quiet - savor it all.

Three: Let Good Enough Be Good Enough

I've always considered myself to be achievement-oriented. It was a tagline on my LinkedIn and a corporate badge of honor - like *"Hey - I give it my best, and I give it my all, all the damn time!"* Maybe because many cultures have defined our worth based on what we accomplish, and the evidence of what we do. It's as if the thought that we might not be doing enough leads to the idea that we might not be enough. Don't be misled into thinking you should be doing more or that what you accomplish has anything to do with what you're worth.

I've had to learn the art of balancing the pursuit of excellence with knowing my own limits and needs. I'm wholeheartedly committed to giving life my best - but I'm also learning to respect my own boundaries, and sense when my body and mind have had enough. In my short thirty-something years of living, I've learned that things will usually fall short of perfection, and to no fault of my own. I've also learned imperfection doesn't make you less than, or inadequate, or insignificant -

it's just life; the way the cookie crumbles so to speak.

To all the perfectionists reading this book: we have got to learn to let good enough be good enough. Stop defining your worth based on what you accomplish, or where you live, or what you drive, or what you wear, or what your parents think, or what your friends think, or where your child goes to school.

Who cares if Suzie's mom baked homemade cupcakes for the bake sale - store-bought is just as good! So what if Bob just brought his husband to Honolulu for Spring Break. Do yourself a favor and *stop comparing your life, and your accomplishments to someone else's highlight reel!* They won't be taking care of you if you stress yourself to a state of sickness. You are doing the absolute best you can and that is enough. Are these words jumping off the page yet? You are enough. So let good enough be good enough!

A good mantra that goes hand in hand with letting good enough be good enough is *"That'll do."* It's a famously brief line spoken by Farmer Hoggett in the film Babe. Spoiler alert: after Babe successfully

herds Farmer Hoggett's sheep at a national herding competition, the Farmer looks down at Babe and says: "*that'll do, pig, that'll do.*" Babe exhales a sweet sigh of relief, knowing he gave it his all. It's the sigh of relief I'm tying this back to.

After you've given the day your best, and given it your all, stop. Remind yourself, "*that'll do.*" It's good enough. No need to keep going, no need to keep pushing. You've done enough, and it's good enough.

Four: It Can Wait

I swear, the moment I turn on my vacation responder, all hell decides to break loose! Folks who never call or text are calling and texting. Clients who are silent all year suddenly want to sign a contract. It's like the moment I decide to step away, all that

I'm pushing and striving for shows up. Well, here's what I have to say to that: it can wait!

That's right.

Boundaries, baby! We've got to be better at creating boundaries in our lives. If you're worried you'll forget something, make a note of it and move on. Let it go to voicemail. You're unavailable. Nothing is so important that it can't wait, unless you really are out there saving lives; in which case may I suggest a trustworthy colleague to back you up while you're unavailable?

Once you've made a commitment to step away or create some time to focus on your own well-being, be sure to respect that boundary. Remind yourself, *"it can wait,"* and tackle it when you're good and ready.

Five: Learn To Say No

No, no thank you, nein, absolutely not. This one quickly became one of my favorite philosophies, mainly because it's been one of the hardest to learn. I've always been a people-pleaser, but unfortunately, it's been to my own detriment.

I've always told myself, *"you can handle it,"* without taking into consideration if my bandwidth was at capacity, or if I had it in me to take on one more thing.

Once you reach your breaking point, you start to take life and all its demands in strides. You get a better each day at knowing your needs, and knowing your limits. When you're at capacity, it's okay to say no.

Don't feel guilty or guilt-tripped into it either. Simply communicate, openly and honestly. Tell folks, *"I really don't have the bandwidth to take this on right now."* If your manager is pressuring you, list out what you have on your plate, and openly ask them what can be taken off the priority list for now. If it's familial obligations or sorting out holidays, sometimes you may just have to miss a Christmas to avoid the stressful, chaotic, traveling with a dog and three kids routine. Folks will understand, and if they don't - oh well.

You have a moral responsibility to your mental health and well-being. Learning to say no is a philosophy that will help keep you balanced and on track.

Six: Take Life One Bite At A Time

Another philosophy is learning to take life one bite at a time. It's the art of being more mindful of what's on your plate. Say you go to a nice restaurant. Your dinner is served, presented ever-so-carefully in front of you. Now, would it be wise to scarf it all down in one bite? That's almost impossible, and kind of gross too. No, you enjoy your meal, one bite at a time. Life is sort of the same way.

To put it in other words: all the things going on around you... you don't have to take them all in, all at once. What's happening *to* you doesn't have to happen *in* you. Does that make sense?

Yes, it's real. Yes, it's happening. Yes, it's stressful. But it's real, happening, and stressful with or without your contribution to it. Sometimes you just have to let things fly all over the place. The dust will settle eventually. The key is not to take it all on or in; and especially don't bite off more than you can chew.

Seven: We Have Two Lives

The seventh and final philosophy comes from a famous Confucius quote:

"We have two lives. The second begins when we realize we only have one."

Different people have different interpretations of what this means to them. Some take it literally, others, metaphorically.

Here's my interpretation: during our first life, we think we have a great deal of time ahead of us, enough to do all the things we want, to love the people in our lives, and take on those projects and passions. Life keeps moving, we get ahead, but not by much. Then one day we open our eyes - likely due to some difficulty we

I encourage you to consider or
this. Out of all the philosophies, this one
has the most potential to change your life.

face - and realize the true gift we have been given. All of the sudden, we want to savor every beautiful moment life throws our way. We find joy in the simplest pleasures. Things that once frustrated us don't even make a mark. We are calm, peaceful, content. Our outlook on life, and on the world begins to change. We discover what matters and learn the art of making each moment count.

Do you feel you live your life in this way? Are your days enriched with joy, peace, and fulfillment? Not to say you've *arrived* but do you appreciate and savor the little things?

I encourage you to really ponder on this. Out of all the philosophies, this one has the most potential to change your life.

Chapter 7

WHERE DO WE GO FROM HERE?

Where do we go from here? Like Confucius said: start living your second life! *How* you may wonder... Do you remember earlier in Chapter 3 when I asked *"who are you?"* I'm sure you came up with a good self-description of your occupation, your roles, responsibilities, needs, and limits. That's great! To take it a step further, do you find joy in all those things?

Let me ask you a different way.

If you woke up tomorrow and absolutely nothing in your life changed, could you be content?

I don't mean that in a defeating sense. Think of it more as: can you find joy in your day-to-day if everything stayed the same? If you were still cleaning dirty diapers, and walking around with throw-up on your favorite blouse? If your co-workers kept complaining about their lot in life? If you never got to those house projects that keep piling up? Could you press on with a smile on your face? Not out of ignorance, but because it's all just okay, and I mean really okay. Not on the outside okay, but in your heart okay.

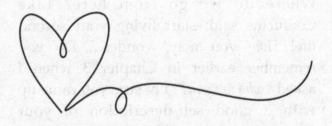

This was such an epiphany for me. The moment I realized that even if nothing in my life ever changed, that all of it - myself included - would be alright. In the big scheme of things, my corporate job was just a job. I would show up, give it my best, and then the day would end. I really do love being a wife, sometimes I was just tired. Rather than becoming frustrated with the responsibilities of daily life, I learned to embrace folding clothes, doing dishes, and cooking dinner too. I found gratitude in having a wonderful man to share my life with, and that was enough. Even though our house chores were a reality, and the to-do list seemed never-ending, *it was all okay*.

The moment I'd start to feel the pressure build-up, that was my queue to put everything down for a bit, and grab onto one of the 12 burnout balancing practices I mentioned earlier. That pressure was my queue to go for a walk outside. It was my opportunity to order takeout for dinner, and go watch the sunset with my husband at the beach. Maybe I'd do a breathing exercise, or grab my notebook and journal for a bit.

No matter which practice I chose, my self-awareness grew to the point where I could recognize burnout creeping up on me, and rather than pushing through it (*like I normally would*), I'd opt to step away and balance it out.

And that's what it all boils down to - acknowledging that we all deserve to have a little more balance in our lives, and then having the courage to take steps toward building it.

Take the First Step

Balance is accessible to all. The first step toward balancing your life is simple. It really begins with your own personal acceptance. You have to be convicted and convinced that balance is as much a necessity for you as any other element. Don't be afraid to invest in your own happiness. You have to honor your body, your mind, and your soul if you're going to sustain your journey in life. The key is knowing that balance is *yours* for the taking.

Having previously worked with women in recovery, I noticed the key to a successful recovery was first found in their willingness to change. The process of balancing burnout is no different. This isn't some self-help mumbo jumbo - this is your health, your opportunity, your big, brilliant, beautiful life. Take it by the helm, and welcome this idea with open arms. Balance belongs to you, and the first step is embracing that fact with every fiber of your being.

Take A Break

Once you've accepted that balance is your right and within your power, take a break. If your schedule permits, take a long break - more of a detox session. I've done it. I'm doing it right now as I write these very words. I ditched my husband for a week, and flew up to the White Mountains in New England. We weren't fighting but we were on edge and needed a little time, a little space, and a little solitude. You see, when you're burnt out, you need breathing room. It's okay to catch your breath... take time to just breathe.

Get to know yourself again. Who are you today, now, at this moment? Understand your needs, and that they may change. Most importantly, learn your limits, and build some boundaries around them. Boundaries are good. Boundaries are healthy. They send a message that you've gone too far, and need to take a step back.

These ideas will teach us the art of our own self-care. Create your own definition of wellbeing, and what it means to you. Value yourself enough to know that you're worth it and you deserve it. It's okay to take a break, especially when you're past your breaking point. In the beginning, take as much time as you need - as much time as life will allow.

Once you feel you've gotten a better handle on things, and are feeling more like yourself, make a personal vow to do this more often. Through time and consistent practice, it's likely you won't need an emergency life-detox session, and will do fine with a personal day sprinkled in here and there. In this sense, you'll be making proactive strides towards a more balanced approach to life.

Find Your Balance

You're confident, you're committed, you're feeling good. You're on your way to balancing burnout in your life once and for all!

I ditched "work-life" and boiled it down to balance a long time ago, because that's what it all comes down to. We find ourselves overwhelmed when things are out of balance. Sometimes we have to pause, take a break, and observe the happenings in our lives. Chances are, if we take time to reflect, we will uncover the culprit that's driving burnout in our lives.

Balance is a personal philosophy, and the secret ingredient to living our fullest lives. From your role as a Mom or a Husband, to a CEO or employee, balance is the secret sauce to contentment, wholeness, and happiness. Once you feel like you've got your footing, and are ready, you can begin again.

Begin Again

And always, we begin again. None of us are perfect. No one has the magic formula, and no one has it all figured out. I'm proud of you though, because the fact that you're still with me reading the words on this page says you're relentlessly committed, and on your way. If I could leave you with some parting advice, please:

Stop comparing yourself to your neighbor, or your co-worker, or that other mom in the pick-up line that seems to have it all together. What we see on the surface of someone else's life is merely a mirage of what they want us to see. Stop comparing behind the scenes of your life with someone else's highlight real. Remind yourself that perfection is an illusion. Accept everything you are, and everything you're not. Accept the parts of yourself that no one else sees, and no one else claps for. Know that there's someone out there admiring you, so let your own light shine. You are beautiful, marvelous, and wonderful - just the way you are. Embrace that.

Be gentle with yourself. You're doing the best you can, and if no one told you this lately, it's going to be alright. I know there's a lot happening in the world, and it's not your fault. Embrace the messiness of your life, because guess what - *everyone's life is a little bit messy*! It's okay. I promise that the dust will settle, the tides will turn, and life will get better. So drop the negative self-talk. Learn to speak to yourself with kindness. Commit to this journey towards better self-care, and discover your own version of balance. You will find your way, I promise!

Take better care of yourself. If there's one thing you gather from the words on these pages, please - please - please, take better care of yourself. You are beautiful, and unique and there is no one out there with your gifts, your talents - or your you-ness. You are phenomenal. Embrace who you are, and where you're at. Listen to your body. Get more rest. Drink more water. Take a nap once in a while. Stop always putting others first - it's okay to love on yourself for a bit too. Drop the guilt of self-care. Drop the guilt of mental health. It's not a taboo or a stigma. You're not sick, you're not selfish, and you're not falling apart - you just need to focus a little more on you, and that's okay.

And, lastly:

Be honest with yourself. Drop the superman act. Ditch your ego for a bit. Be honest with yourself. Know who you are, and love who you are. Ask for help when you need it. Take a break when you feel it's time. Accept the messiness of your life - as a matter of fact, embrace it. It's okay that you don't have it all together. There is power in vulnerability, and more power in acceptance. Honesty requires courage; I know you have it in you. Stop worrying about things you have zero control over. Make a vow to live your truth, and live it fully.

And that's all I have for you, for now. I wrote this book to inspire, and encourage those of you who are searching for balance in your life. Remember - balance is personal. It's relative and individual and intimate. No two people will discover balance the same way - and that's alright. Discover your own version, play with it, dissect it, make it your own. You deserve to experience the fullness of life with a happy heart, and head held high. Cheers to your journey!

With love,

V

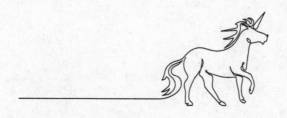

BIBLIOGRAPHY

1. NCBI. *Depression: What is burnout?* June 18, 2020. https://www.ncbi.nlm.nih.gov/books/NBK279286

2. Science of People. *How to Fight Burnout and Get Unstuck in 11 Empowering Steps.* https://www.scienceofpeople.com/burnout

3. WebMD. *What are the consequences of long-term stress?* Reviewed by Jennifer Casarella on August 1, 2019. https://www.webmd.com/balance/stress-management/qa/what-are-the-consequences-of-longterm-stress

4. Bible.org. *Meaning of the Unstrung Bow.* Our Daily Bread, June 6, 1994. https://bible.org/illustration/meaning-unstrung-bow

5. Harvard Business Review. *The Busier You Are, the More You Need Quiet Time.* Justin Zorn + Leigh Marz. 3/17/2017.

https://bg.hbr.org/2017/03/the-busier-you-are-the-more-you-need-quiet-time

6. The Breath Effect. *9 Amazing Facts About Breathing*. Emma Ferris. 12/26/2018. https://www.thebreatheffect.com/facts-about-breathing

7. Yale Environment 360. *Ecopsychology: How Immersion in Nature Benefits Your Health*. Jim Robbins. 1/9/2020. https://e360.yale.edu/features/ecopsychology-how-immersion-in-nature-benefits-your-health

ARTWORK

Mihail © Adobe ID 368478674

АнастасияКулик © Adobe ID 246802595

Olga Rai © Adobe ID 429771271

Oleksandr © Adobe ID 295675731

ngupakarti © Adobe ID 415712211

Gondex © Adobe ID 276332503

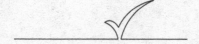

LuckyStep © Adobe ID 431494911

GarkushaArt © Adobe ID 288333525

Mihail © Adobe ID 360005564

ngupakarti © Adobe ID 231830827

art_of_line © Adobe ID 455639517

RedlineVector © Adobe ID 112226546

ABOUT THE AUTHOR

Vanessa Autrey is the author of *The Art of Balancing Burnout*, her first book in a self-help series. Now a full-time writer, Vanessa and her husband share their time between Saint Petersburg, Florida and the White Mountains of New Hampshire.

For more details, you can visit:

www.vanessaautrey.com